JOSEPH MIDTHUN   SAMUEL HITI

BUILDING BLOCKS OF SCIENCE

SOUND

WORLD
BOOK

a Scott Fetzer company
Chicago
www.worldbookonline.com

World Book, Inc.
233 N. Michigan Avenue
Chicago, IL 60601
U.S.A.

For information about other World Book publications, visit our website at http://www.worldbookonline.com or call 1-800-WORLDBK (967-5325).

For information about sales to schools and libraries, call 1-800-975-3250 (United States); 1-800-837-5365 (Canada).

Library of Congress Cataloging-in-Publication Data

Sound.
        p. cm. -- (Building blocks of science)
     Includes index.
     Summary: "A graphic nonfiction volume that introduces sound energy. Features include several photographic pages, a glossary, additional resource list, and an index"--Provided by publisher.
     ISBN 978-0-7166-1430-2
     1. Sound--Juvenile literature. I. World Book, Inc.
  QC225.5.S665 2012
  534--dc23
                            2011025978

Building Blocks of Science
Set ISBN: 978-0-7166-1420-3

Printed in China by Leo Paper Products LTD., Heshan, Guangdong
1st printing December 2011

Acknowledgments:
Created by Samuel Hiti and Joseph Midthun.
Art by Samuel Hiti. Written by Joseph Midthun.

© sciencephotos/Alamy Images 10, 24; © Trevor Smith/Alamy Images 17; © WoodyStock/Alamy Images 17; © Taxi/Getty Images 16; © David Gunn, iStockphoto 25; Shutterstock 11

ATTENTION, READER!

Some characters in this series throw large objects from tall buildings, play with fire, ride on bicycle handlebars, and perform other dangerous acts. However, they are CARTOON CHARACTERS. Please do not try any of these things at home because you could seriously harm yourself—or others around you!

STAFF

Executive Committee
President: Donald D. Keller
Vice President and Editor in Chief: Paul A. Kobasa
Vice President, Marketing/
   Digital Products: Sean Klunder
Vice President, International: Richard Flower
Director, Human Resources: Bev Ecker

Editorial
Associate Manager, Supplementary
   Publications: Cassie Mayer
Writer and Letterer: Joseph Midthun
Editors: Mike DuRoss and Brian Johnson
Researcher: Annie Brodsky
Manager, Contracts & Compliance
   (Rights & Permissions): Loranne K. Shields

Manufacturing/Pre-Press/Graphics and Design
Director: Carma Fazio
Manufacturing Manager: Steven Hueppchen
Production/Technology Manager:
   Anne Fritzinger
Proofreader: Emilie Schrage
Manager, Graphics and Design: Tom Evans
Coordinator, Design Development and
   Production: Brenda B. Tropinski
Book Design: Samuel Hiti
Photographs Editor: Kathy Creech

TABLE OF CONTENTS

There is a glossary on page 30. Terms defined in the glossary are in type **that looks like this** on their first appearance.

Sound comes from objects that vibrate.

When something vibrates, it moves back and forth.

SOUNDS CAN BE LOUD!

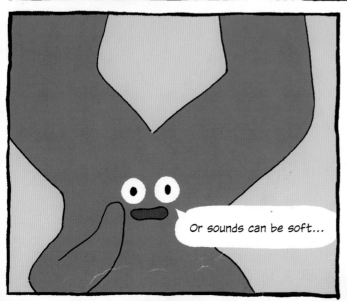

Or sounds can be soft...

But there is more to me than meets the ear!

5

When an object vibrates...

...the air around the object vibrates, too!

These vibrations in the air are called **sound waves.**

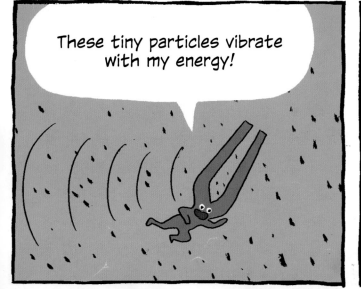

What happens once a sound reaches your ears?

Let's take a look inside!

ZIP

Sound waves enter your ears and hit the **eardrum.**

PLOP PLOP

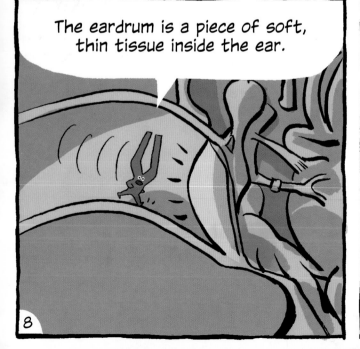

The eardrum is a piece of soft, thin tissue inside the ear.

It stretches across the tube inside your ear.

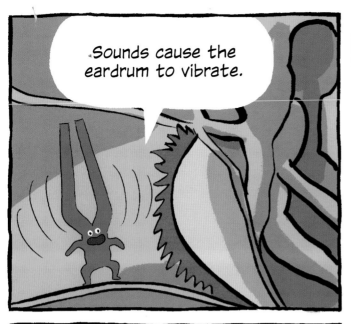

Sounds cause the eardrum to vibrate.

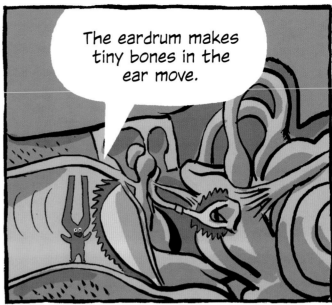

The eardrum makes tiny bones in the ear move.

These bones send the sound to a curled tube deep inside the ear called the **cochlea.**

The cochlea is full of liquid. As the sound waves travel through this liquid, they make tiny hairs bend.

The bending hairs cause nerves to send signals to the brain.

Auditory cortex

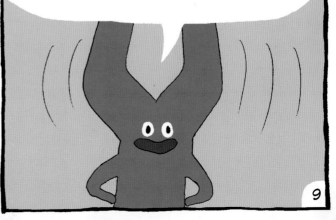

Your brain uses these signals to perceive sound.

CARRYING SOUND

Sound can move through any **state of matter**—gas, solid, or liquid.

But I travel faster through solids and liquids than I do through air.

That's because the particles in solids and liquids are closer together than the particles in air.

Listen!

You can probably hear a sound coming from somewhere right now...

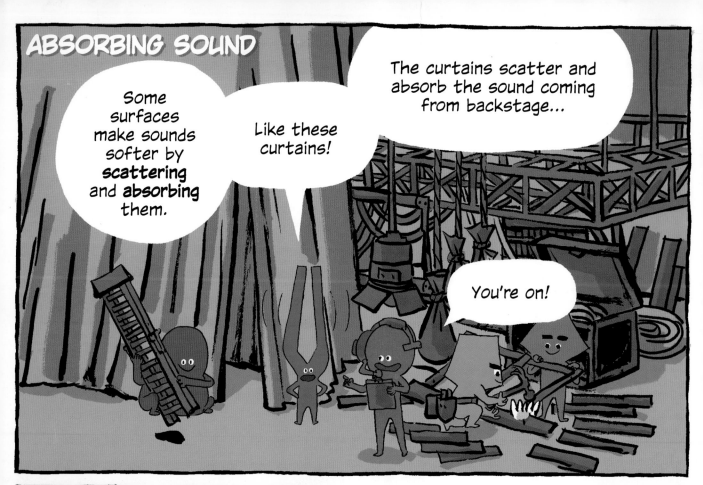

Some places need more sound absorption than others.

Recording studios, opera houses, and dance clubs are all built with sound control in mind.

In this concert hall, the seats are cushioned to absorb sound.

Even if the seat is empty, it absorbs as much sound as if someone were there.

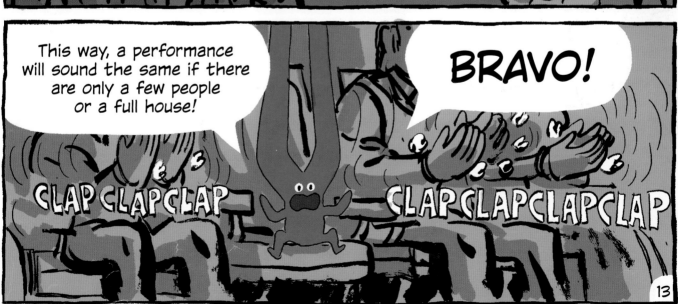

This way, a performance will sound the same if there are only a few people or a full house!

BRAVO!

CLAP CLAPCLAP

CLAPCLAPCLAPCLAP

WHAT MAKES AN ECHO?

Some surfaces **reflect** sound. When sounds reflect back at us, we may hear an **echo.**

For example, when you shout, the sound of your voice travels through the air in all directions.

You hear the shout when the sound first reaches your ears.

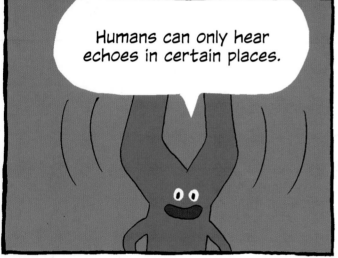

Humans can only hear echoes in certain places.

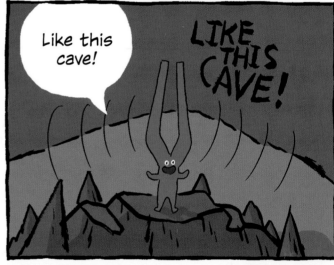

Like this cave!

LIKE THIS CAVE!

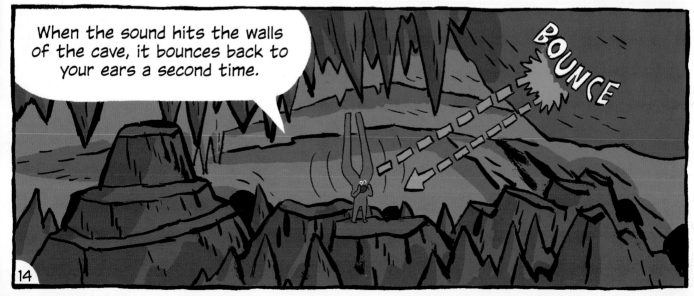

When the sound hits the walls of the cave, it bounces back to your ears a second time.

BOUNCE

Animals with better hearing than humans hear echoes all the time!

Some animals use echoes to navigate and hunt. Bats, dolphins, and whales all use **echolocation.**

ECHOLOCATION ECHOLOCATION ECHOLOCATION

A bat can "see" in the dark with sound.

SWOOP

Look out!

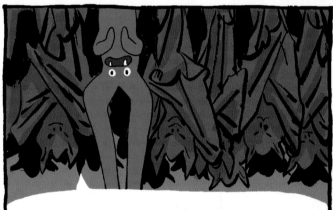

Bats make a high-pitched sound and listen to the echoes that are reflected back.

Then the bat can measure the **distance** to a cave wall or even a tasty snack.

Dolphins and whales use echolocation to sense objects and other sea creatures.

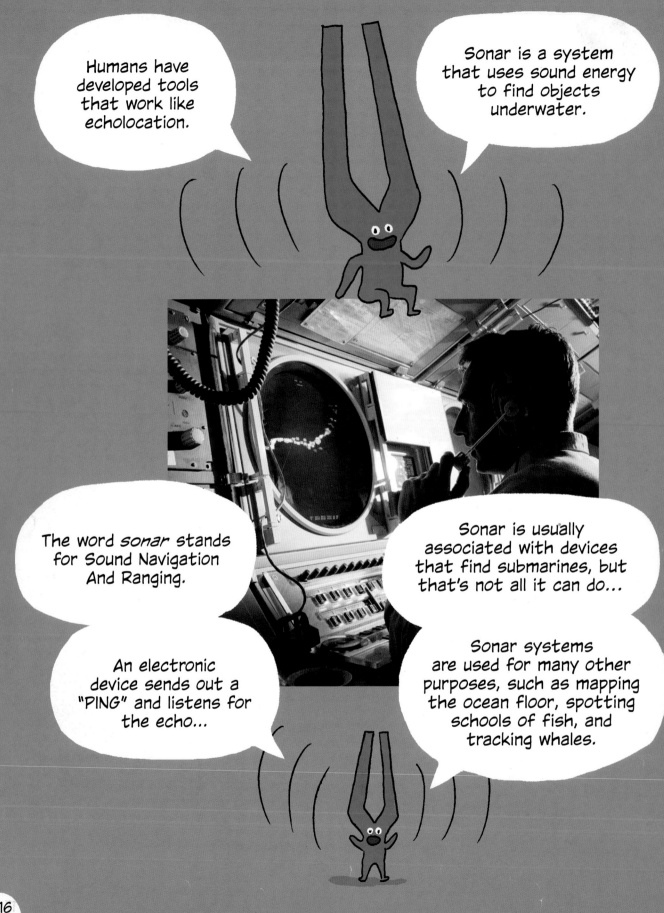

Some burglar alarms use **ultrasound** to detect movement.

Ultrasound is a type of sonar that operates at a frequency above human hearing.

Doctors can use an ultrasound machine to take a peek inside your body!

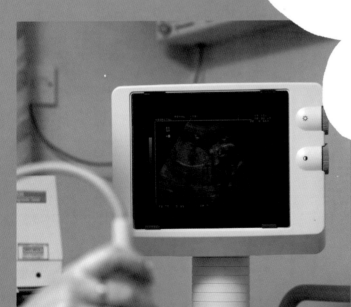

SOUND WAVES

The shape of a sound wave can tell us about the quality of the sound.

Sound waves are somewhat like ocean waves.

They have high points and low points.

The high point of a sound wave is called a **crest**, or peak.

The crest represents the area of crowded particles in a sound wave.

The low point of the sound wave is called a **trough**, or valley.

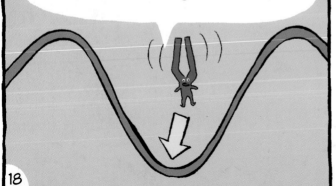

The trough represents the area in a sound wave where the particles are farthest apart.

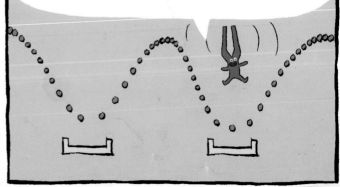

Sound waves are even more similar to the coils in a toy spring.

Watch what happens as this toy spring moves down the stairs.

The coils push together and spread apart.

The coils of the spring that are bunched together are the crests of the wave.

The coils that are spread apart are the troughs!

The greater the amplitude...

...the more energy in the wave...

AMPLITUDE

THE LOUDER THE SOUND!

Some sounds you can barely hear at all...

Like a pin drop!

Ping

Soft sounds have less energy than loud sounds.

HOW HIGH OR LOW?

Sounds can be high...

And sounds can be low.

Have you ever wondered what makes a sound high or low?

It has to do with **frequency.**

Frequency is the number of sound waves that pass a point in a given time.

TIC TIC TIC TIC TIC TIC TIC TIC TIC TIC

The faster an object vibrates, the greater its frequency.

Frequency determines **pitch**—how high or low a sound is.

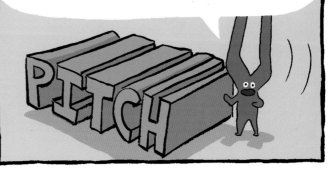

High-pitched sounds have a higher frequency than low-pitched sounds.

The growl of a lion is a low-pitched sound.

A songbird's call is a high-pitched sound!

ROAR.

chirp.

23

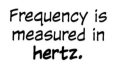

Frequency is measured in **hertz.**

You can measure frequency on an oscilloscope!

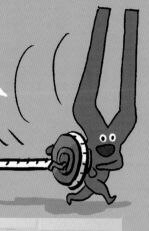

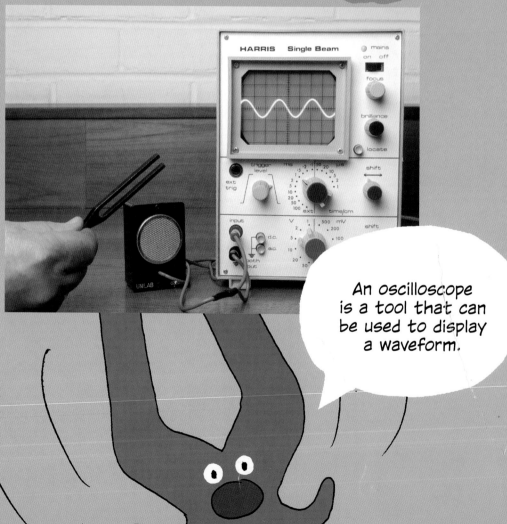

An oscilloscope is a tool that can be used to display a waveform.

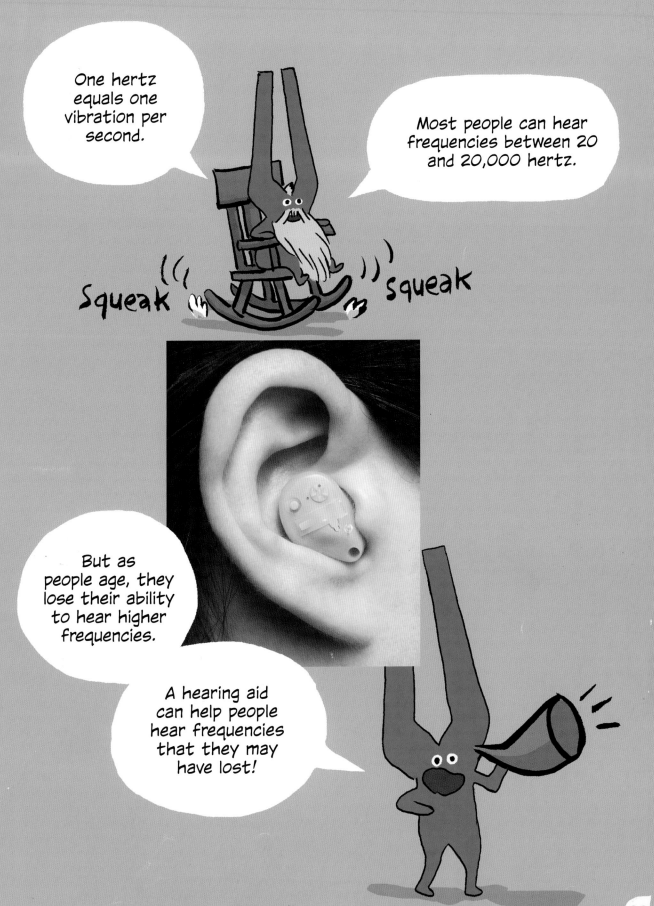

One hertz equals one vibration per second.

Most people can hear frequencies between 20 and 20,000 hertz.

Squeak squeak

But as people age, they lose their ability to hear higher frequencies.

A hearing aid can help people hear frequencies that they may have lost!

Many kinds of animals can hear sounds with higher or lower frequencies than a human can hear.

Elephants can coordinate their movements through low-frequency sounds and vibrations that are communicated through the ground!

This way, if they become separated, they can find each other.

This whistle makes a high-frequency sound that humans can't hear.

Dogs can, though!

Some animals can hear much softer sounds than people can.

A barn owl can hear the footsteps of its prey.

This allows the owl to hunt in complete darkness.

SWOOP

27

People have been studying sound since ancient times.

Today, scientists use their knowledge of sound in many ways.

Ultrasound can be used to clean delicate instruments!

It can also be used to help heal wounds and injuries.

With sound, humans are able to map the floor of some of the deepest parts of the ocean!

Scientists have used sonar to discover vast underwater plains, mountain chains, and volcanoes.

And these are just a few uses of me...

Maybe you can come up with a brand-new use for me!

Hear ya 'round!

I'm *SOUND!*

GLOSSARY

absorb to take in and hold rather than reflect.

amplitude the amount of energy in a wave.

cochlea a spiral-shaped cavity of the inner ear.

crest the highest point of a sound wave. The crest represents the area where particles in the wave are crowded together.

distance the amount of space between two points.

eardrum the part of the ear that vibrates in response to sounds.

echo a reflected sound.

echolocation the use of sound by certain animals to sense their surroundings. Bats and dolphins use echolocation.

frequency the number of sound waves or light waves that pass by one point in a given time.

hertz a unit used to measure sound frequency. One hertz equals one cycle (sound wave) per second.

pitch the highness or lowness of a sound.

reflect to throw back light, heat, sound, or other form of energy. Reflection occurs when energy or an object bounces off a surface.

scatter to separate and drive off in different directions.

sound wave energy that moves through a material, such as air or water, as a vibration.

states of matter the different forms of matter. The most familiar are solid, liquid, and gas.

trough the lowest point of a sound wave. The trough represents the area where particles in the wave are spread farthest apart.

ultrasound sound that is too high-pitched for human beings to hear.

FIND OUT MORE

Books

All About Sound by Lisa Trumbauer (Children's Press, 2004)

Bangs and Twangs: Science Fun with Sound by Vicki Cobb and Steve Haefele (Millbrook Press, 2000)

Hearing by Nick Winnick (Weigl Publishers, 2010)

Light and Sound by Steve Parker (Raintree Steck-Vaughn, 2001)

The Science of Sound and Music by Shar Levine and Leslie Johnstone (Sterling Publishing, 2000)

Sounds All Around by Wendy Pfeffer and Holly Keller (HarperCollins, 1999)

Sound: From Doppler to Sonar by Christopher Cooper (Heinemann Library, 2003)

Sound: Loud, Soft, High, and Low by Natalie M. Rosinsky and Matthew John (Picture Window Books, 2003)

Websites

Changing Sounds
http://www.bbc.co.uk/schools/scienceclips/ages/9_10/changing_sounds.shtml
Use the interactive tools at this website from the BBC to play around with sound.

Exploratorium: Science Snacks About Sound
http://www.exploratorium.edu/snacks/iconsound.html
Simple experiments let you play with sound and its effects at this educational website.

The NASA SCI Files: Sound Activities
http://scifiles.larc.nasa.gov/text/kids/D_Lab/acts_sound.html
"Dr. D's lab" provides plenty of opportunities to experiment with the science of sound.

NeoK12: Sound
http://www.neok12.com/Sound.htm
Videos at this site take you through the basics of sound science, from waves and resonance to how the human ear works.

NOVA Online: Faster Than Sound
http://www.pbs.org/wgbh/nova/barrier/
Read all about sonic booms and the people who first broke the sound barrier at this site from NOVA.

The Sound Site
http://www.smm.org/sound/nocss/top.html
Explore the world of sound at this educational, interactive site from the Science Museum of Minnesota.

Try Science: Experiments
http://www.tryscience.org/experiments/experiments_home.html
At this site, experiments such as Hilarious Honker and Mysterious Melodies let you explore sound and pitch.

ZOOM Sound: Listen Up
http://pbskids.org/zoom/activities/sci/#sound
Use the science of sound to build your own instruments at this website from PBS Kids.

INDEX

32